# Make Money With This "Affiliate Marketing Secrets!"

Congratulations and thanks a lot for buying this affiliate-marketing guide!

It's my honest hope that you will learn a lot about affiliate marketing and how you can make good money through it.

Feel free to rebrand this eBook with your affiliate links plus some added info and give it away to make profits; just make sure you reference it! You can also use this information on your website or print the book as a hard copy.

Visit my website at https://www.joshonline247.home.blog now to sign up for more free materials and information to rebrand and give away on your website or sell; go ahead to build a mailing list and earn some easy profits!

I0402273

## Legal Notice

The author has strived to be as thorough and accurate as he could when creating this eBook. He has put all efforts to ensure that information provided herein is verified and exact. Nevertheless, because of the rapidly changing nature of the internet, he doesn't guarantee at any time that the information in this book is accurate. The publisher is not responsible for any faults, omissions or contrary interpretation of the theme. The book is not aimed for use as a source of business, accounting, legal or financial advice and all readers are advised to seek knowledge from competent specialists regarding the relevant fields.

## Copyright Notice

All content contained in this eBook is secured by copyright and may not be reproduced or rebranded without the consent of the author. To enhance easy reading, you are encouraged to print this eBook. You can also use the content of this book on your website, blog, email newsletter, videos, and social media posts, as well as anywhere else you may wish.

## Material Connection Disclosure

You ought to assume that the publisher and author of this eBook have an affiliate and/or another material connection with the providers of services and goods cited in this book and may (or may not) get compensation if you buy from a provider through the links provided. You should always do an intelligent research before purchasing goods or services from anyone whether offline or online.

# Overview

This book is for you if your primary goal is to earn passive income with little effort and time, as well as little or no capital. It will guide you how to create a business that is self-sustaining and reliable.

It is aimed to help any person hoping to improve their revenue, especially if you have no experience in the affiliate marketing industry. It offers a clear, straightforward and detailed info regarding the essentials required to make constant passive income through affiliate business.

The book enlightens you on how to go about the affiliate marketing business and prosper as a merchant or affiliate. It gives you the role of affiliates and merchants in the business and even shows you how much you can earn with this business.

According to reviewers, this book has the ability to change your perception on affiliate marketing by tying in various aspects of this business. Ryan covers all the fundamentals and techniques of successful affiliate marketing from social media, to SEO and email marketing.

It clearly explains the types of affiliate marketing programs and how each works, then gives you the best recommendation to upsurge your income. This is the reason why this book is recommended for both newbies and experts in this business. It even goes ahead to explain the benefits, cons and myths about affiliate marketing, thereby giving you a clear understanding of how this business operates.

If you are a beginner in this business, this book will fully equip you with more knowledge and understanding than what you are searching for. You will come back to this book even after you have mastered the art of affiliate marketing. If you are an expert, you will be able to see the potential of your business from a different perspective.

Ryan gives 50+ best affiliate-marketing platforms to join and make real money in 2019. In addition, he gives 30+ blogs and websites to follow in 2019 to enhance your knowledge on affiliate marketing.

While it explains clearly the affiliate marketing trends in 2019 and beyond, it also guides you on what to and not do, the frequently asked questions, how to select a lucrative niche, how to get started and drive targeted traffic to your affiliate links in order to succeed in affiliate marketing business.

## About the author

Josh Ryan is a proud eBook author who grew up travelling, earned a bachelor's degree in Sociology and currently working in the online business world. He is experienced and loves writing since young age. He loves to be resourceful and helpful to those he meet locally and online. He is always absorbed by music, especially reggae music. He believes in and acknowledges the power and blessings of the Almighty God. He is a fan of generosity and helping those who need him with whatever he has – ideas, materials, and other things. Josh loves the greens and fruits, as well as a glass of hot coffee in the evening. He has two brothers, three sisters, one wife and one truly loved son. Currently, Josh lives in Canada with his family and Jackie, his beloved dog pet.

# Table of Contents

### 6.2.2 Best affiliate marketing blogs to follow in 2019

# List of abbreviations

CPS - Cost Per Sale

CPL - Cost Per Lead

CPC - Cost Per Click

CPA - Cost Per Action

CTA – Call To Action

CTRs – Click Through Rates

ISP – Internet Service Provider

LSI - Latent Semantic Indexing

PPC – Pay Per Click

ROI – Return On Investment

SEM – Search Engine Marketing

SERPs – Search Engine Results Pages

SEO – Search Engine Optimization

URL – Uniform Resource Locator

# Chapter One: Introduction

## 1.1 What is affiliate marketing?

Everyone want to get this passive income through affiliate marketing.

This is where you promote other people's (or company's) products through an affiliate network and earn commissions when people buy the product through your link. Publishers/merchants share their revenues with marketers who triggered the sales.

In affiliate marketing, you can be either a merchant or an affiliate marketer.

If you have one or several products and want to increase the sales, you can let the marketers assist you in promoting your products and give them with a little share of the sale price.

If you don't have your own products, worry less because you can be an affiliate marketer. Go ahead and choose the products that feel valuable to you, promote them and wait for income to flow as sales rise.

Earning as a marketer depends on the number of sales you make, which depends on your marketing skills. There is no limit to your earning as an affiliate.

However, whichever route you choose is capable of bringing you hundreds or millions of dollars each month.

Now, let's dive deeper into what affiliate marketing really involves.

Affiliate marketing can be said to be a process of spreading product creation and marketing across distinct parties, where the revenue is shared among the involved parties depending on their contribution.

There are four parties involved in successful affiliate marketing, including the following:

### 1. The merchant

This is an individual or a company that creates brands and sells the product. This party doesn't have to be actively involved, as long as it has a product to sell.

### 2. Affiliate

Also known as the publisher, affiliates are individuals and companies that promotes and markets one or multiple products to attract the potential customers and convince them to buy the products.

You can use your blog if you have one, create an entire site and dedicate it solely to reviewing the products or use other techniques such as social media marketing. Either way, you will earn commissions on every sale you make.

**NB:** You can be both a merchant and an affiliate and end up earning huge amounts of income through affiliate marketing.

### 3. Consumer

This is the most essential part of affiliate marketing. Without the consumers, there are no sales and consequently, no revenues to be shared. Consumers get attracted (through social networks, digital billboards or a blog) to purchase merchant's products and once they do, both the merchant and affiliate earns some revenue.

**NB:** Affiliates choose whether to inform the consumers that they are part of the affiliate marketing system or not.

### 4. Network

This is not always considered as a part of the affiliate marketing system. However, networks works as crucial intermediaries between the merchant and the affiliate. They simplify the payment and delivery process, and track the source of the sales so that both the affiliate and the merchant can earn their genuine revenue.

In most cases, merchants manage their affiliate programs through certain networks. Then, the marketers get the links/banners/images from the affiliate networks and promote them. They get their share of revenue for each sale made through their affiliate links.

The affiliate network holds a huge collection of products from different merchants. They allow marketers to join and generate affiliate links to the different products. Once sales are made through the affiliate links, the marketer gets some commission.

In the end of this book, I have compiled a bonus of 50+ affiliate networks you can join NOW and start making money as an affiliate.

But still, it is vital to know how this whole this thing works. So, continue reading.

## 1.2 Who can do it?

Affiliate marketing can be done by anyone who has the passion of making passive income online. Would you like to make these silent revenues? If yes, then you can do it. Remember you have the potential of doing anything you decide.

Once you have set the goal of becoming a successful affiliate marketer, make sure you have a reliable internet connection since everything will be doable online. A computer would greatly help you to browse for research as well as marketing the affiliate reviews. Therefore, you might need some basic computer knowledge.

However, affiliate marketing is not a tough thing for those who believe in themselves. Just give it a try, pick some affiliate links and write reviews for them. Drive traffic to these review pages and videos and then wait for potential customers to purchase the product through your links, after which you get a certain share of revenue per sale.

You should understand that anyone can do it and you are not exceptional. Believe in yourself and look for the highest converting affiliate links from your affiliate networks, then start promoting them to earn some reliable passive income.

## 1.3 How much can you earn with affiliate marketing?

Actually, there is no limit to earning with affiliate marketing since everything depends on sales made, which may vary from time to time for different products.

As a merchant, you can earn hundred dollars or up to several millions in one year depending on the number of sales you make. For example, let's say you are selling a simple product (like an eBook) for US $5. If you make a thousand sales for this product in one month, you will have earned $5,000 from that one product. What if you have 20 products costing around the same price and you sell 1000 copies of each product? Then you will earn 20x1000x$5 = $100,000 that month. Crazy amount? Think about it. In a year, you will have made a revenue of $1,200,000.

To earn this money as a merchant, you need to make your products stand out from the rest in their categories. You need also to make sure you market and advertise your products, and connect with affiliates through different networks to increase your sales.

As an affiliate, you can make huge income through affiliate marketing business. Your earnings depend on your marketing skills and traffic sources. If you drive good number of well-targeted traffic to the merchants' sales pages, you can make millions of dollars in a very short time.

You need to convince the potential customers on the features and benefits of the specific item you are promoting. Let them know the good things that the product will help them do or will do for them. This could be through a well-explained video or informative blog post. Then, you can get traffic for these resources by using paid advertising to reach more targeted audience. Once the audience have read or watched the whole blog or video consecutively, there are high chances that they will be influenced and click the buy button you have added at the bottom. And once they buy, you have your share of revenue.

For example, a product may be paying you $3 commission for each sale you drive. If you make them a thousand sales in one month, you'll have made $3,000. What if you make a thousand sales for twenty different products? That will bring you $60,000 revenue in a month. In one year, you will have made $720,000. This is amazing, right?

To increase your earnings, you need to promote a big number of high-converting products. Use good advertising techniques to drive more traffic to your review materials and then wait for the passive income to flow. You can make millions of dollars per year as an affiliate marketer; you just have to be cautious when you decide to try it. In addition, don't give up too soon; good results may not show immediately, but with continuous efforts, they will definitely show.

That is to say that you are the only limit to the amount of your revenues. Do what others are doing, join the networks that are famous in supporting your niche, and you will soon be a good example of a successful affiliate marketer or online merchant.

## 1.4 Tools and skills you need to start affiliate marketing

To start as an affiliate marketer, there are no many tools and resources needed. Just the basics. Have a computer and a reliable network. That's all! Then, create a YouTube channel and/or a website where you will be sharing your review videos and posts. You can create social media accounts such as Facebook, Twitter, Tumblr, Pinterest, among others and use them to distribute your review materials to a larger audience.

Additionally, you need a way to collect emails from people interested in your niche, who are the potential buyers of the products you are promoting. You will learn more about this in the **steps to becoming a successful affiliate marketer in chapter 2.**

At the same time, you may need to have good research skills so that you can find the highest-converting and well-paying affiliate links from the best affiliate networks or merchants. Promoting products with high conversion rates and from trusted merchants/networks increases the potentiality of directing more sales and earning more revenue.

Good skills are researched or learned, and most of internet users are likely to have this skill; it only need to be directed to the niche of your interest.

All the above will help you to start and progress towards success in affiliate marketing. Dedication is not a thing to be forgotten as in any other income-generating activities. Use your time well; plan your actions with an aim. To guarantee yourself some good constant passive income.

## 1.5 Fundamentals of affiliate marketing

Affiliate marketing needs not to be intimidating or hidden in a mystery. Rather, it should be clear and understandable even to those who are new in this industry. The basic principles of affiliate marketing are naturally sensible and align with the number of businesses that have operated since the beginning compared to those who have evolved to the online marketing.

It is a kind of performance-based marketing where the affiliates get rewarded with commission by a seller for a successful sale directed through their referral links. Basically, this in not very distinct compared to the traditional times where salespeople would earn commissions after driving in successful sales or sign ups.

Below are the fundamental principles of affiliate marketing:

1. Choose a niche. When selecting your niche, decide on a topic. You need to search online to ensure that your niche is not saturated already. In case you find it saturated with well-designed and high ranking websites, consider finding another niche. I will explain how you can choose a lucrative niche later.

2. Look for affiliate networks that offer the products or services that fit your niche. Such networks include Clickbank, JVZoo, Amazon, among others. I have a list of these at the last chapter of this book; you can jump ahead and look- if you like.

3. Practice good keyword searching. You can get a wide diversity of keyword tools from the internet, some for free and others at reasonable prices. In addition, a variety of blogs and tutorials that explains how to use these tools is available online. Use them to your advantage. Efficiently research the best-converting keywords. In most cases, several long tailed keywords are preferred in every page you create, but don't overuse them.

4. Create a website. Choose a theme and get a developer design a website for you. As well, you can get web hosts that offer themes and plugins to fit your needs such as WordPress, so that you just go ahead and start posting. There are even some web hosts that offer free hosting and so, you can easily set up one fast.

5. Provide high quality and unique content on your website, while requesting comments at the end. Information related to your niche is already out there, so it's upon you to twist and improve the topics, adding complements and solving the issues others may have made. Additionally, ensure that the titles are attractive and shareable, the content is awesome and everything revolves around the keywords.

6. Below or in-between the review posts, share your affiliate links so that the readers can buy the product if the comprehensive information they just read impresses them. However, don't make a mistake of sharing affiliate links on every post as this would saturate your site. Do this only if your website specializes on product reviews, like the TopTenReviews.com does. You should include other great information and guidance in the site to increase your ranking.

7. Distribute your posts through social media networks to inform the world of your freshly published pages and videos. While posting, make sure you add some caption text along with the URL to your page or video. In addition to making naturally sharable posts, you can get your friends help you share the posts across the networks, or even use PPC advertising.

8. Send your newly published posts to your email subscribers and urge them to forward the emails to others who they think might be interested.

These are the most essential basics of affiliate marketing. You only need to join a good merchant or affiliate network and promote the products they offer using the above principles. This will help you succeed as an affiliate marketer as soon as you start.

## 1.6 Types of affiliate marketing programs

Affiliate marketing programs can be broken down into three main categories, which shows explains how different people make affiliate income through the program. They include the following:

- Unattached
- Related
- Involved

Let's dive deeper into what these programs entail.

**Unattached Affiliate Marketing**

This program includes paid advertising and the affiliates has no presence or authority in the niche of the product they are promoting. As the affiliate, you are not directly connected to the final consumer since you are presenting your affiliate links to the audience through advertisers such as Facebook ads, Google AdWords, among others. You earn a commission when the audience clicks your affiliate links and buys the products you are promoting.

However, this type of affiliate marketing is not very attractive since it lacks authority and presence of the marketer. This could instill fear on the minds of the audience and make it somehow hard to lead successful sales. Additionally, it gives you no way to build a relationship with the end user. You act as a behind-the-scenes middleman between the sellers and final consumers.

Nevertheless, it's not a very simple method of earning good income as it's hard to build trust and confidence with your audience. But if it does, well and good, I wish you continued success.

**Related Affiliate Marketing**

This is a form of affiliate marketing, where you have some online presence through a blog, YouTube channel, social media networks, podcasts, etc. and promote affiliate products **related** to your niche. It is not a necessity that you have experience in using these products, you just have to write a good comprehensive review explaining the features and benefits that comes with the products.

Once you have online presence, you can look for traffic for your materials in which you have put the affiliate links. When your visitors read your detailed review, they might be interested in buying the product(s) you are promoting, thereby earning you some commissions.

People are most likely to trust you when you place the affiliate ads on your website, channel, or page than when you have none. You can use banners or text ads at the sidebar or below the posts. Make sure you put them somewhere that your audience will easily find them.

**Involved Affiliate Marketing**

Here, you recommend a product or service that you have already used and proved to be both beneficial and reliable. You take your time to write good detailed content regarding the characteristics of certain product(s) or service(s) from your experience. It is not very advisable to put the links somewhere like "recommended resources" or just in a banner, rather, include them within or below the content.

Your experience and involvement with the products you are promoting attracts your visitors since they understand the advantages and functionalities of the products. Therefore, they are much likely to purchase the products through your affiliate links, thereby earning you great revenues.

In case you have a huge influence over your followers, you are somehow responsible while making these types of recommendations. Be honest and provide helpful information from experience, and you will influence many people to buy the product you are promoting. Hence, you generate more affiliate income.

Those are the three major types of affiliate marketing and you should choose the one that works best for you. However, I would advise you to use the third type in which you have some presence and authority in your niche and recommend the products that you have benefited from in one way or the other.

You should always focus on building good levels of confidence, trust and genuineness with your audience. First, emphasize on serving your audience and then income. Offer them what is best for them.

Be fully involved in affiliate marketing and believe me, success will be yours to enjoy. Keep reading on to find out how affiliate marketing really works.

# Chapter Two: How does it work?

Affiliate marketing works through a collaboration of the above four parties, each playing a crucial role in the entire process.

## 2.1 Role of the Merchant

The merchant creates the product, brands it and passes it on to the affiliate network. To become a merchant or product creator, you need to follow these four steps:

### Step 1: Come up with a product idea

It is not easy or a necessity to come up with a new idea in the market. However, you can look at the products that are already available and the problems their users are experiencing. Then, come up with ways to solve the problems as you improve the performance and functionality of the product.

### Step 2: Validate your idea

This helps to ensure that your idea is good and admirable to the people. You could just create the product and throw it to the market, but if people don't like it, then it will be hard for you to make cash out of it.

To validate your idea, ask people whether they can pay money for it. You can post the idea on "Topsy" and ask people whether they would be interested in it. Go ahead and ask them to place orders if they would like the product. After receiving a good number of orders, you can now proceed and create the product.

### Step 3: Create the product

Depending on your investment budget, you can choose to create a physical or digital product. Digital products are the best way for newbies since they generally need your time and little or no money only.

After creating the product and delivered to your first customers, you can go ahead and open up the affiliate network.

### Step 4: Find affiliate program partners

To raise the number of sales and revenues in turn, you need to find affiliate partners or networks that will connect you to the marketers, who will promote your product. The networks also help in collecting revenue from your product's sales. Some examples of these networks include Gumroad, Digital Product Delivery, Amazon, etc.

The important part is to find a person to collaborate with and help you find an audience interested in your product. Commissions and other details can be added later after **getting started.**

Nevertheless, remember that you can just become an affiliate and promote your products yourself.

## 2.2 Role of the Affiliate

Once the product has been created and posted on the affiliate network, the affiliate marketer comes in and starts promoting the product. As an affiliate, join the network and promote the affiliate links to start earning commissions. Attract and convince customers to buy the specific products, after which you get rewarded.

In order to become a successful affiliate marketer, simply follow the below **four steps**.

### Step 1: Review products in your niche

This is where you publicly talk about the products you like, have used, or any other products you are promoting. You can use a blog, YouTube channel or live streams through Periscope to tell people about the outstanding features and benefits of different products.

There are numerous products available in distinct affiliate networks that you can pick and start promoting. To get started, look for the products in which you are interested. Trust me, any product will work.

Proceed and review the products on your YouTube channel or blog, showing how it works, its unique features, as well as its benefits. You can also review the top ten or best products in your niche. Whichever the case, use affiliate links to direct your readers/viewers to the affiliate pages where they can buy the products. Once they buy the product(s), you will earn some amount of commission.

However, relying on people to use the affiliate links in your reviews may need a lot of traffic to earn you good money. You should look for a way to contact them directly, not necessarily when they visit your blog or channel. That is when you proceed to the next step.

### Step 2: Build an email list

Email is one of the best marketing channel in the online world. Identify ways to collect emails from your web visitors. You can add subscription forms and attract people to join by offering them a good thing free in exchange of their email address. For example, you can give them a free eBook or a special video.

You need to keep your audience engaged by sending them updates on a regular basis, such as once per week. Make sure you don't sell on each email. You can just inform them of new posts and reviews.

Note: Even if your email list has below 500 people, you still have the potential to make considerable sales and earn good money.

### Step 3: Use live webinars to educate your audience

Webinars are greatly known for the way they help affiliates and other web publishers to instantly engage with their audience. They allow you to show the audience detailed information regarding certain products that you are promoting. This may include the history and present features of a product, how it is used, as well as its pros and cons. At the same time, your audience is able to get the most out of it and even get answers to any questions that they might be having.

By the end of the webinar, your audience will be so excited for knowing the suitability of the product you are reviewing. If you point or share your affiliate link at the end, people are most likely to go ahead and buy the products in the affiliate network. This is after seeing you spending about an hour explaining about the product. You won't have forced them since they will freely decide to buy the product if it suits them.

A soft sell!

**Pro tip: Y**ou can ask for a special deal or discount for your audience from your merchant. To do this, you just need to promise the merchant that you will get their awareness of their product to a good number of people; may be a hundred or more. In most cases, they will be happy to give you a special bundle or price cut to help you influence more people to buy.

### Step 4: Get traffic to the review pages/videos that you created

Getting people to view or watch the review videos and pages that you created is the only way that has the potential to get you sales and revenue. This is because, it is after reading a detailed positive review or watching a well-explained video regarding the product, that the consumers will get interested to purchase it.

The following tips will help you drive targeted traffic to your affiliate products' reviews:

## 2.2.1 How to get targeted traffic on your website/blog

### 1. Create great content

Ensure that you dedicate enough time and effort to craft truly resourceful and incredible content. When the post is engaging and attracting, adding a buy button at the end will be beneficial to the readers, rather than being harmful. In addition, great content has the potential to influence more visitors into buyers, thereby earning you more revenue.

### 2. Practice operational SEO techniques

It is necessary to utilize good and effective SEO strategies in order to drive quality traffic from search engines. To rank among the best results links in the search engines, you need to use more keywords naturally within your great content. Long tail specific keywords tends to rank higher than one-word or short keywords.

To enhance the ranking, consider skyscraping where you find the best content for your specific keyword and use it to create your own. Make it unique and better than the original by expanding the topic or covering the areas that might be missing from the original content. High ranking on search engines means more targeted and potential consumers of the products you are reviewing.

## 3. Paid Promotion

As soon as your affiliate marketing business begins picking up, you can start practicing paid advertising. In the end, conversions are all that matters and it doesn't matter where the traffic come from.

Most successful affiliate marketers pay to get traffic through platforms such as Google AdWords, Facebook Ads, among other advertising networks. I recommend using social networks and search engines to get traffic to your promotion pages.

When you use Pay-Per-Click (PPC) advertising, you get a high chance to:

- ✓ Get targeted audience for your webinar.
- ✓ Grow your email list.
- ✓ Increase your sales.

The best PPC advertisement is promoting sign-ups to your mailing list or webinar. This is because, once you have the emails, you can regularly inform the subscribers of new posts and product reviews. You can even put them on an automated email sequence designed to encourage them to buy the products you are promoting. Email marketing can earn you tons of dollars when integrated with affiliate marketing.

**Wise note:** Engage in PPC advertising only if you have a way to get back your money.

## 4. Promote products that you would purchase

It can be extremely difficult nearly impossible to persuade your audience to buy something that you yourself would not like to purchase. Therefore, it is highly recommendable to promote products that you are passionate about or somehow interested in. This will help you to come out clearly and give your audience comprehensive information and benefits of the products you are promoting. Then, make the review as engaging as possible and coax the readers/viewers to purchase the products.

Once you have traffic, you will start directing sales through the affiliate links and you will be rewarded for it. For every sale you make, there is a certain percentage of share that will be given to you by the merchant, may be through the affiliate network(s).

The more the traffic, the more the sales you can potentially make and therefore, the more the revenue. So, focus on driving traffic to the review videos, webinars and the webpages you created.

## 2.3 Strategies (or secret) for successful affiliate marketing

As you may already know, affiliate marketing is not that easy. That's why most people give up only a few days or months after starting it. Because obviously you can't keep adding effort to something that's not bearing the anticipated fruits. Those who make it know a secret not known by many and practice certain strategies that help them succeed in this business. Here I have compiled a list of **seven** best and proven strategies to gear you towards your success as an affiliate marketer.

### 1) Look for a unique niche

Many affiliate marketers make the mistake of trying to offer everything available in the market rather than focusing on a particular niche. When you focus on a one specific and profitable niche, there are high chances that you will gradually grow in your brand awareness, trust, reach and even conversions. You can choose a niche from the known profitable ones such as wealth, health, and romance. Decide on a niche and put all your focus on it through informative posts and promotion reviews.

### 2) Choose the right affiliate partners

If you want to be good in influencing consumers to buy products through your links, it's advisable to work with trusted affiliate networks. Customers are likely to buy more if they know (or heard of) the merchant or seller of the products. The right affiliate partners will ensure that neither their services nor the products do not disappoint your referrals. This consequently increases your conversion rates and therefore you earn more.

### 3) Search Engine Marketing (SEM)

After designing your website and filling it with distinct kinds of content, promoting it will help you reach a larger audience. Many of the affiliates use PPC advertising such as Overture, Google Ads, Facebook Ads, among others, but this could be a bit expensive for the starters. However, driving traffic organically to your site is very effective as there is high likeliness of getting genuine traffic. Use on-page techniques, and an impressive easy-to-navigate and high-converting website design to boost your SEO. You can also consider SEM companies to help improve your SEO. This will prevent you from spending tons of your profit on PPC advertisements.

### 4) Know your audience and products

Your website should be a great resource for consumers. That's why you need to learn more about both your target audience and the product and services you are promoting. This improves your credibility when creating content and hence you get more trusted by your followers. If they trust you, they are more likely to trust in your reviews and purchase through your links, and your revenues rise that way.

### 5) Promote product from diversified merchants

Always ensure you promote products from various sellers within your niche. This helps to ensure your business doesn't suffer even if one or more merchants delay their payments, or their products have low conversion rates. You are responsible for your progress and definitely, promoting products from diverse merchants will reduce chances of famine impact in case something does not go as expected.

## 6) Never stop learning

As you may possibly know, the world of affiliate marketing keeps on changing day in day out and strategies might get outdated any time. So, its wise to keep searching for knowledge and trends in this industry. Try to learn something new regarding affiliate marketing on a daily basis. Be prepared to embrace changes for the better. Know what others are doing to succeed and do it yourself. You will soon join them in the world of successful online marketers.

## 7) Never give up

Most people try affiliate marketing and lose hope soon if they don't see positive results immediately. Before you start, design a good blueprint of how everything will be done and set realistic achievable goals. Upgrade where necessary. Note that, success never comes in a nightshift. But with continuous efforts, you will start earning better revenues.

Others have made it. And so should you. Take your time to choose a good niche that will be both converting and profitable, may be with less competition. Then, strategize on how you will achieve your dreams. Act tirelessly and after some time, you will be among those called successful affiliates.

## 2.4 How to Find a Profitable Niche in Affiliate Marketing

In the journey of affiliate marketing, choosing a niche is one of the most intimidating phases. However, it's importance can't allow us to overlook or rush through it. It helps you to join a strong market of buyers that has a bit less competition. Whether you are new to affiliate marketing or not, the steps below will help you select a niche in which you can become a winning competitor.

### 1. Do a comprehensive research.

Do a thorough research on sites like Qauntcast.com to know the most popular niches in the internet world. Look for the ranking of different niches to identify the ones that are doing great. As you scroll down the ranking list, you will be able to find more niche-directed sites such as travel, wealth, among others. This will help you realize the types of audience targeted by these popular niches as well as more topic ideas.

### 2. Brainstorm and break down the idea.

You can head over to a crowdsource site like Quora.com, Yahoo Answers, among others that provide questions and answers related to your niche. Search your broad niche idea and break it into smaller niches from which you can create websites and promote affiliate offers on them. For example, you can break down a "travel" niche into a more specific one such as "The greatest beach vacation," "Favorite travel destinations to visit before you die," and many more. Make sure you brainstorm for different niches from the main wide one. In case you feel as if it isn't working, revisit Qauntcast and other such sites to see what the broader niche entails. Once you have selected a specific niche, go to the next step, which is:

### 3. Checking it's monetization on ClickBank

Here, you take your selected niche topic and test its value. The niche needs to have monetization capabilities so that you can drive sales from the traffic you have. Otherwise, there is no point in diving into affiliate marketing if the niche is 'hard' to monetize. I recommend ClickBank as it's a great site with huge numbers of users and therefore, it's likely to have most of the available niches.

To get started, go to the affiliate marketplace from the top menu of the platform. Sort the products by "Gravity" or use the top search bar to search for your niche category and narrow down the search. You will get product results that you could sell for your specific niche. Observe and investigate whether there is availability of products that are easy to sell in your niche.

In case you are not getting any good results, just repeat the procedure until you find natural products that will be a bit easy to sell.

### 4. Check the CPC for keywords in your niche

This is another essential step to take when finding the best affiliate niche. Double-check the promotions of that niche's keywords on sites like AdWords. This will help you realize the level of competition in the niche you selected.

Try to search related keywords in your niche from which you can write content and drive traffic and sales.

Base the search on certain categories, enter your search terms and hit the "Get ideas" button. You will get the average monthly searches, competition as well as suggested bids. The monthly searches will help you know the amount of traffic gotten by these keywords. The competition will let you understand how hard it will be to rank for them. Then, sort the search by suggested bids to see the niches with many marketers willing to pay good amounts for each click.

If someone is ready and willing to pay huge cash for a single click, it means that there are high-value affiliate products to promote for these niches. It shows that there is high ability of these niches to produce significant results even in one click.

You can go back to ClickBank and search again to try to narrow your search further. This way, you will have found yourself a lucrative niche.

5. **Look for affiliate opportunities for the selected niche**

After finding a profitable niche, you need to search for affiliate product opportunities so that you can be sure to make money from that niche. Find affiliate programs related to your niche and join them; most of them are free. Some examples of best affiliate programs for consumer goods may include Amazon and ClickBank. Choose the best products that will fit to promote on your website.

## 2.5 Question to ask yourself before deciding on a niche

Sometimes, the niche you desire may not always convert into huge revenues. This is because other people may not be passionate about the same thing as you. So, before you start writing on a niche that you are passionate about, make sure even other people will want to know even more. To know whether a niche is profitable and fit for you, you might need to research and ask yourself the following questions:

1. **What is the level of demand in this niche?**

You can use the **Google Keywords Planner** tool to check the search volume data of the specific keyword(s). This will help you to know the number of people searching for topics in your niche. You might want to consider a niche with high demand levels so that you can be sure to get traffic once you start posting.

2. **What are the trends in your niche?**

You need to know whether your niche is in stable, growing or dying trend. To do this, you can find the niche's data on the Google Trends. You should ensure that the niche you selected is growing and evergreen throughout the year, rather than seasonally.

3. **Are there marketers selling products in the niche?**

Visit online markets such as eBay or Amazon to check whether people are selling products related to your niche. Consider the volume of items sold throughout a year. Check the feedback score of the products to see if they are bestselling in the market. In addition, you can look at the Watch Count to see the popular products that are being watched.

4. **Are there plenty products promotable in the selected niche?**

Use data from affiliate networks such as Amazon Associates, ShareASale, Panthera Network, Clickbank, among others to see the availability of affiliate products to promote in your specific niche. If any niche has a great number of buyers and affiliate products, it can be profitable.

If you get positive answers for the above questions, then you have found yourself a favorite and profitable niche to write on. Promote the products in that niche and am sure you will start selling with time.

## 2.6 What next?

It is crucial to choose a niche that you like and is full of high-selling products that you can promote. Once you have selected a favorite niche, it's time to go onward and conquer. Proceed to writing informative and engaging posts and product reviews. Then, use the social media, SEO and email marketing tactics to drive traffic to these pages. Get affiliate links and promote them on your website to start earning from the successful sales you drive there. Next, I am going to show you the best social media, SEO and email marketing strategies that will help you generate highly converting traffic and make the most out of your affiliate marketing business.

# Chapter Three: Affiliate Marketing Strategies

After finding a quality affiliate product to promote, you can evade the many work hours used in coming up with a persuasive product and creating a high-converting sales page. To earn revenues, simply drive traffic to a promotion that converts. Using social media, SEO and email marketing techniques, you can start to make good income through affiliate marketing.

## 3.1 Social media affiliate marketing tactics

This is where you promote your affiliate links or product reviews by distributing them through social media platforms such as Facebook, Pinterest, Google+, Stumble Upon, Tumblr, Twitter, among others. Social media marketing is one of the leading marketing techniques used by affiliates and website owners to drive traffic to their affiliate links and websites or blogs.

If you get an affiliate link and share it directly on social media, it might be difficult to get plenty traffic and sales. This is because there is no place for you to explain the benefits the buyers will get and the value of the product you are promoting. Some social media platforms such as Facebook tries to exclude sales related posts from the news feed. This means that when you post your affiliate link there, it will not preview appropriately.

When you don't promote your affiliate links properly even on other social medias, there are high chances of getting low traffic results and hence, less or no sales and income. However, here I have compiled a list of six ideas to help you get maximum results from social media so that you can create more impact and value, thereby increasing your affiliate earnings.

### 1. Start by providing brilliant quality content

This is the first step when it comes to successful affiliate marketing. Produce and share high quality content that your audience will enjoy. Do not ALWAYS promote products and services on the platforms. Rather, deliver convincing content and then include your affiliate links at the end of the content.

You can compile your content in a social media or blog post, email newsletter, infographic, YouTube video or a podcast. Whenever possible, try to purchase and use any product you are promoting. This makes it easier for you to genuinely recommend and promote that product to other people using quality content and your affiliate link. Add opt-in forms on your website for people to join your email list easily. You can also use a light-box plugin to capture subscribers.

## 2. Smartly generate affiliate redirect links.

For many people nowadays, fresh affiliate URLs are easily spotted due to their sketchy looks and therefore don't click them. This is why it is very important to turn the fresh affiliate links into more friendly redirected links. Look at this row link:

http://ad9719fta-dp4w1fpisqhl1v25.hop.clickbank.net/

It appears unfriendly and have unclear destination and therefore, people are not likely to click it. However, you can create a cleaner redirect link that attracts more people to click it, such as:

https://joshonline247.com/MIL/

If you are using WordPress self-host, you can easily set up this using the Redirection Plugin provided.

There are various link shortening websites most of which do not allow use of affiliate links. For example, bit.ly, goo.gl, etc. don't allow ClickBank hop links. However, the tinyurl.com does. Make sure you are smart in shortening your affiliate links to impress your social followers and drive you traffic & sales.

## 3. Use images of the product you are promoting.

As you may probably know, pictures attract clicks. When you are promoting a certain product, the merchants mostly provide photos of the products. Use these pictures on your social media posts and other posts, and then attach your redirect affiliate links so your audience can buy the items if they like them.

## 4. Grow your subscription list with social media.

This is the best way to get most out of your social media. Social media platforms sell advertising space and works to maintain high quality content on their websites. Therefore, if you promote affiliate offers on these sites, you are risking the banning of your account. To mitigate this risk and increase the conversion rates, it's advisable to build a targeted email list. Having a big responsive email list means more traffic and more revenues. Provide great content freely to build trust with your audience. Then, respect that trust by recommending only high quality services and products.

In case you use Aweber mailing service, you can automatically set your broadcast emails to post on your Facebook page and Twitter stream.

## 5. Promote high quality deals only!

To make money with social media affiliate marketing, it is crucial to promote only the products that are high quality. This is the best strategy of affiliate marketing since each party wins. The customer wins by obtaining awesome deals on excellent products and services. As the affiliate, you win by earning good commissions for referring successful sales. And the merchant wins by selling more products. Basically, high quality offer promotions are advantageous to all.

6. **Set up timeless auto-responder emails.**

Email auto-responders such as Mailchip, Aweber, Mailerlite, among others are powerful tools for turning new subscribers into honest readers who will hit the affiliate links and consider the products you recommend. You can set up to 7 auto emails to send one daily for the first seven days once someone joins your list. Also, you can turn these emails into an eCourse that attracts people to join and stay in your list. And eCourse is much valuable to depict about your emails being high quality from the beginning.

(If you use email marketing tools like xMails, you will be able to send unlimited emails to unlimited subscribers just with one click. xMails provides you with numerous email templates so that you don't have to do the hard design work all by yourself. Check the xMails review on my website at https://www.joshonline247.home.blog/ to see if it will help you achieve your email marketing dreams and earn tons of cash.)

Using the above techniques, you can get great results from combining social media with your affiliate marketing business.

## 3.2 SEO affiliate marketing tips

Search Engine Optimization (SEO) refers to the way a website is optimized in order to rank high in search engines such as Google, Yandex, Bing, among others. As an affiliate, it is crucial to have good SEO practices so that you can rank high and convert many visitors into buyers of the products you are promoting. And an increase in sales means increase in revenues.

However, the link between affiliate marketing and SEO can be complicated. In such a case, most affiliate networks conclude that their rankings lower due to poor practices of one or several affiliates. To fight this bad reputation of affiliate backlinks, it is crucial to have clear understanding of good SEO practices for affiliates. This starts by knowing the criteria used by search engines in ranking websites.

Once you have practiced good SEO techniques, your site will reward you with more revenue. Below is my breakthrough about the best effective SEO marketing tips for successful affiliate journey.

**1) Select your niche**

This is one of the most important stages of affiliate marketing. Once you choose a niche that suits you well, you are half the journey. I have explained above how to choose a good high-converting niche, so am hoping you have the knowledge. Make sure you can find a variety of keywords related to your niche. After selecting a good niche, go ahead and get yourself a domain name.

## 2) Choose your domain name

A website's domain name also determines whether the site will be a successful one. You can choose to get a large authoritative website that you can later brand. At the same time, you can decide on a short, simple and straightforward name. Come up with the long-term goals for your site before launching it. This will help ensure your site has the potentiality of succeeding and bringing you huge income.

I recommend choosing and building a huge authority website. This is because you can be on top all times and make real cash. However, selecting an exact match domain and targeting a single major keyword could eventually fail with changes in trends.

## 3) Decide on a good website host

May be you are asking, does hosting really matter? Yes! Hosting plays a crucial role in generating traffic regardless of the method you choose - PPC, SEO, and Social Media marketing. If a host is slow in loading, then your site will be slow too. Whichever method you use to drive traffic, they will soon leave if your site takes too long to load a single page. This negatively affects the efforts you had put to drive the traffic and your revenues can even lower to zero.

With a good website hosting solution, the website will load faster, the connection secure, reliable, local and inexpensive. You can look for customer reviews and ratings of different hosting companies before deciding which one to use. Just be sure your choice is a reliable one.

## 4) High-quality content

For your site to rank high, you need to provide high quality and detailed content, which will largely be determined by the choices you made earlier. Ensure you create seriously amazing content that engages, educates, entertains and adds value to the reader. This will definitely attract more backlinks and this means higher ranking. You should also ensure that your content is comprehensive and long to at least 1500 words for blogs- best SEO perspective since 2016. The video and presentation content should also be long enough and thoroughly researched.

High quality content will increase the trust and loyalty of your audience, thereby enticing them to purchase the services or products you are promoting. This is the best way to attract high rankings on search engines and this means loads of targeted traffic and possibly more revenues. If done right, SEO can attract huge numbers of followers and regular readers ever.

## 5) Right keywords' selection

The keywords you choose for your niche and posts directly affects your SEO ranking. It's recommended that you choose a short and memorable domain name so that your URL can be short. Google values the first five words of your domain more than the others do. It introduced Latent Semantic Indexing (LSI) and added the Hummingbird Algorithm to its search engine. This ensures that the engine figures out what your post is actually about.

To ensure high rankings, ensure you use long tail keywords that have less competition. Due to LSI, you don't have to keep repeating the keywords or writing them as they are. This makes long keywords stand out from short ones.

For example, instead of using highly competing keywords such as "best restaurants," you can use long tail keyword like "best Italian restaurants in Virginia." Make sure your keywords are closely related to the products you are promoting.

To enhance optimization, you might need to use LSIgraph tool. It is a very easy and comfortable to use tool so you will do your keyword research efficiently.

### 6) Do on-page SEO

No matter the size of your website, on-page SEO should be ensured on every page. Make sure you occasionally include the target keywords within your article, page and subpages. Also, use them on the title of the page as well as alternate names for included images. Each page might require different optimization from the others if they are not directly related (e.g. in case of a wide authority website). However, you need to ensure you do the following on each specific page or post.

- The **main keyword density** should be about 1.5-2.5 percent of the whole content. This helps Google to easily understand the relevance of your website to this keyword or topic. Main keywords also have a commercial significance, so ensure you use them along with other informational keywords to support your sales posts even via other pieces of content. For lucrative affiliate marketing SEO tactics, try to consider the purpose and nature of the keywords while assigning them to articles.
- **Using appealing introductory paragraph** is a great way to captivate your audience. Therefore, always ensure that your initial paragraph is powerful and attractive to hook your audience right from the beginning. This lowers the bounce rates and boosts your articles' ranking on search engines.
- **Use H1/H2/H3 titles** for different sections of your articles. Ensure you use the main keyword in the H1 heading. This gives your visitors an easier time reading when reading your content. Additionally, it assists Google in understanding what a certain article is about.
- **Ensure you put 'alt' tags containing keywords.** Make sure that all your images have alt tags that comprises keywords. To understand what an image is about, Google bots are pointed to the alt tags. So, make better use of them to increase your ranking.

### 7) Include more media and CTAs.

While writing your articles, try to add media and call to actions to make it easier for your readers to understand all the information contained. In this case, you may decide to use images, embedded videos or infographics. Good videos and CTAs assist in boosting the activeness and engagements of your site visitors. You can use Google Analytics to get reports that are more detailed regarding this performance. Distributing them wisely enhances the rankings since Google identifies it as a positive user experience.

## 8) Ensure your site is mobile-responsive

A mobile-responsive website responds quickly in a clear design on all types and sizes of mobile devices. With the increase in number of mobile users, optimizing your site for mobile is very essential. According to projections, more than 80 percent of online users and about half of online traffic comes from mobile devices. That being said, you need to ensure that your site is mobile-friendly (if you haven't already). If you use site builders such as WordPress themes, you can use plugins to help you optimize for fast, easy and clear mobile browsing. You can find services from sites like Google PageSpeed Insights for testing and solutions to increase loading speed.

## 8) Ensure good Social Media practices

In the world of online marketing, there is no doubt that social media is the king. Most people use different social media platforms to communicate, share and read peoples thoughts. To promote their brands and establish effective communication with world audience, over 95% of affiliates and online merchants some kind of social media marketing campaigns.

Using different interactive platforms makes customers feel like they are communicating with others rather than connecting with an impersonal company. Use it to engage your followers and occasionally recommends products to them, or redirect them to your site where they can read the comprehensive post you have written. When used appropriately, it can attract high conversions. And remember, the post will ever be seen by your growing audience. When the post is great, people will comment on it, share and promote it for you, thereby enhancing your brand awareness.

## 9) Optimize your site for conversions

If your website is not well optimized for conversions, all the above points will be meaningless. Even though you need to get traffic to get conversions, ensure that you dedicate the necessary time (and/or money) to add good CTAs. This helps to direct viewers where you want them to go. No matter how small twists you make, you can start getting massive conversions and profits.

Affiliate marketing is an awesome method for anyone to make money online from anywhere. You become your own boss, work the time you want and best of all, allows you maximum freedom since you don't have to keep working; it gives you passive income. It's not easy though, but it's not a very hard work. With help of the above SEO and social media marketing techniques, you can start reaping the fruits of affiliate success.

## 3.3 Email marketing tips for affiliate marketing

Email marketing is an incredibly powerful tool for distributing information to your prospects and website followers, and driving highly targeted traffic to your affiliate links. send the emails occasionally and make sure you don't mercilessly spam your subscribers. It helps you strengthen the relationship with them, always reminding them to message you when they need.

Marketing emails are educational and promotional messages sent to people who requested you to keep updating them such as clients, vendors, prospects, affiliates, reporters, etc. They can contain different types of content including newsletters, announcements, sales promotions, surveys, press releases, and follow-ups.

It is good to optimize your email to attract more opens and click rates. With good email marketing services and tactics, you can improve your website's traffic and generate more sales, hence more money. Now, let's dive into the tips to help you improve your email marketing efforts.

### 1) Build your email list

No matter how many addresses you have in your email list, always try to add it even more. You can use signup forms on your website, blog, or anywhere else where you trigger your visitors to drop their email so that they get an added advantage. Obviously, it may not be easy to convince someone to give you their email if you are not providing value to them. So, try to come up with a free give-away such as an eBook or other valuable information that will entice more people to subscribe. You can also add popup signup forms at different levels of page scrolling. If you clearly and precisely describe the value of subscribing, you are very likely to turn your visitors into subscribers.

### 2) Personalize your emails

At all times, try to add personal elements when sending out your emails. Make your recipients feel your presence by using a nice salutation that includes the recipient's name. Ensure you use creative subject lines and personalized content. Be fast and efficient in responding to the subscribers' email replies. You can also group your email lists into different categories of your audience and send them different versions of your email.

### 3) Provide high-value content

For effective email marketing, you need to give your audience something that helps or provides them with genuine solutions. To make them stick to your business, provide relevant information such as marketing messages about the products you are offering, operational info about the services you provide, or educational information related to your industry. This helps you build trust with your subscribers and your messages do not go to their trash folder.

### 4) Inspire your readers to reply

Email marketing enhances meaningful conversations between you and your subscribers. You should not just send them any information, rather one that helps them in a way. To ensure your audience opens the emails and enhance replies, ensure you use irresistible subject lines while speaking directly to your readers. Offer and promise something outstanding from other emails in their inbox.

In addition, ensure you use an amusing and unique voice to make it sound real and caring, rather than a machine-generated message. Always send targeted emails by segmenting your lists according to different demographics and interests. This way, your readers are more likely to open and read the email, reply and even forward it to other friends and prospects.

## 5) Include exciting links with calls to action

Email affiliate marketing is aimed at increasing traffic to a product reviews or affiliate links. When there are no clicks to the pages, it means there are no sales. It is crucial to add visually eye-catching calls to action buttons with some text to inform the readers of an interactive opportunity to look at, such as Get it now! Learn more...! Get instant access! Download now! among others. Describe them well to entice your readers to perform specific actions. Then, include your affiliate links as hyperlinks under these CTAs to direct the traffic to the merchant's sales page to earn commissions on successful purchases.

## 6) Ensure your emails are mobile-friendly

Many people are using mobile phones in everyday activities, more than computers. According to reports, 66+percent of emails are opened on smartphones and tablets. It is therefore essential to optimize your emails for mobile and other small-screened devices. Ignoring this practice can make you miss out numerous clicks, and you don't want that.

## 7) Make your emails look crunchy and clean

To some, this may sound very obvious. However, many people send emails that look like shoddy and outdated websites of the twentieth century. You should ensure your emails contain information relevant to the engaging subject title. Also, ensure that you use keywords relevant to your readers' interests and use short paragraphs. You can use bullet points and illustrative images to ease skimming and a better understanding of your message.

## 8) Ease the opt-out process

Always make it easy for your subscribers to leave the list. This may look as if you are declining the conversation, but it is a free will of the subscriber to stay or leave. It is better they sign out than flagging your emails as spam, as this could bring you troubles in the future.

## 9) Test the emails before distributing them

Before you send your emails, make sure they display properly on all devices and that they look exactly the way you want them to look. View them on Yahoo, Google, and Outlook.com, and using different devices. You can use tools like Litmus for stronger testing. In addition, make sure that all the included links and the personalization shortcodes work correctly. In case these look wrong, you will look very unprofessional and imprudent.

At the same time, experiment your emails with different subject lines, body texts, calls to action, and even on different days of the week. You can run your own tests or use A/B split testing modules provided by most email tools to compare the results of various versions of your emails. This will help you realize the most engaging content type to your audience that attracts highest response rates.

## 10) Track your emails

Sometimes, results do not depend on the content type or platforms' optimization. Always analyze your data to know the deliverability of your emails and the opening times. Such information can help you realize the performance of your emails. In case you use Google Analytics, you can tag emails with custom campaign tracking to see their rate of driving traffic on your website as well as the behaviors of the traffic they bring. This information can help you tailor your messages to people who will benefit from it.

## 11) Do not devastate your subscribers

Maybe you are anticipating starting using these tips in sending out as many emails to your subscribers as you can. However, be cautious how frequently you send your emails so that you don't flood their inbox with promotional messages regarding all your offers. This may irritate them and even make them unsubscribe.

## 12) Prevent your emails from going to spam folders

Sometimes you construct your emails carefully and they still end up flagged as spam. First, ensure that your email receivers have opted into your email lists. Avoid overusing caps and exclamation marks. In addition, use properly formatted HTML codes in your emails so that the email service providers can handle them correctly. Test to ensure your emails pass through all filters before disbursing them. This way your emails will reach the inbox as soon as you hit the send button or when the scheduled time arrives.

Those are flawless tips for effective email affiliate marketing. Follow them and send your emails occasionally, only when truly important. However, succeeding in affiliate marketing through the email strategy is not an easy task. It requires good planning and analyzing your data to adjust your campaigns. Effective email marketing attracts more traffic when done right, which attracts more sales and revenue. If you want to learn more about email marketing, start emailing now!

# Chapter Four: More About Affiliate Marketing

## 4.1 Top mistakes done by affiliate marketers

When SEO, email and social media are used together to achieve preset affiliate marketing goals, this business can be really powerful and lucrative. However, many marketers fail to do these important parts and ignore the SEO marketing or other mistakes. These consequently affect the effectiveness on your campaigns. Avoiding these mistakes can have long-term positive impact on your traffic and sales. Below are the top 10 mistakes done by affiliates.

### 1) Focusing on keywords rather than solutions

Many affiliates make the mistake of plugging keywords on their landing pages without considering the importance their products have on the customers. Rather than aiming more on solution provision, many people focus more on the keyword density. You should include main keywords integrated severally in the article to attract high traffic but only use them as a base. Make sure your content is informative and helps readers to solve a problem through a successful method, such as purchasing a certain product.

### 2) Depending on affiliate business as your only revenue stream

Rather than considering it as a revenue channel, various affiliates mistake by treating affiliate marketing as a business model. Affiliate marketing is a revenue channel for monetizing your website, but try to use other methods too- such as Google AdSense, AdWords, etc. Diversifying your income networks helps ensure you still earn even if one method fails.

### 3) Producing plagiarized rather than original content

Many affiliate websites copy content from other sites and slightly edit it, then attach product lists and publish the posts. This consequently lowers your ranking on Google and other search engines. You should always write unique and really valuable content for your visitors as it helps the search engines to rank your site high for relevant keywords. Note that most of the sites with duplicated content never rank well, therefore you need to add value and quality for search engines to rank your site high.

### 4) Lack or duplicating Meta descriptions

In most cases, you may find affiliates misusing or not able to write good convincing titles and Meta descriptions. You should ensure that your listings are unique and relevant to the keywords/topics. A simple recommendation would be taking the first paragraphs of every page and put them as the Meta descriptions of each specific page. You might want to consider plugins such as Yoast SEO if you are using WordPress. They work very well for on-page SEO and helps you create custom Meta description templates. Another plugin would be SmartCrawl, which generates Meta descriptions for you in an automated manner.

Using unique Meta descriptions that are related to the main keyword will help your affiliate pages rise up high the SERPs thereby making you stand out from your competitors.

## 5) Overlooking Mobile Optimization

Many of the affiliate websites appear horrible on mobile devices. This makes them lose the opportunity to outdo other brands in mobile SERPs. The biggest problems with SEO for mobile is low speed, normally caused by unused plugins and images, as well as ignoring optimization of site for AMP version. If you give your users a faster experience while browsing through the valuable engaging content on your site, you can be able to outrank all your competitors. I recommend prioritizing mobile optimization for high mobile conversions and sales.

## 6) Use of free web hosting solutions

Nowadays, there are various sites such as Wix, WordPress, etc. that provide free and paid hosting solutions. Many new affiliates make the mistake of free solutions, making their business seem somehow unreal. When using free hosting, you do not own the site architecture and you have limited control over things that boost rankings. Always try to own your website, data and content to protect yourself and your visitors.

## 7) Use of irrelevant backlinks

For successful affiliate business, backlinks assist in bringing new visitors as well as the ranking of your site. However, irrelevant backlinks can easily get you in trouble with Google since they may be seen as "link schemes" with more negatives than benefits. In order to prevent this, make sure all your affiliate pages add significant value to any person who visits them. Ensure that your backlinks are hosted on authoritative sites to prevent them from devaluing your site's ranking.

## 8) Using undefined canonicals

When you use canonical URLs, they assist you in improving link and ranking indicators for your website content. You should organize your site into various categories, which you use to communicate to your audience. Canonical URLs assists a lot in managing the content on your affiliate site as well as improving your ranking signals. To learn more about them, you can visit Google Search Console page that gives more information that is detailed.

## 9) Act as if the best SEO practices do not apply to affiliate site SEO

Most affiliates normally ignore common SEO mistakes on their site. This includes 404 errors, broken links, thin and duplicate content, excessive redirects issues. All these mistakes need to be addressed to ensure good crawlability and health of your site. You can download a complex suite of SEO tools that can assist you to check and eliminate any errors, as well as correct any problematic content.

Though good SEO needs more work, its rewards are really worth it. Work to clean up your site internally, ease the navigation and speed, and advance your crawl budget. To the search engines, your site is no different from the merchant or other sites. It is valued based on what you offer your visitors. So, always ensure you do the regular site cleanup and maintenance.

I advise you not to undervalue the effect of SEO on your affiliate marketing business. They are very crucial in determining your site's rank on SERPs. Try to avoid the above mistakes and you will be a step ahead towards the high ranks. You can use PPC advertising to attract early leads to your new affiliate site but it's wiser to grow the site naturally by cultivating strong organic links to boost conversions through good SEO.

## 4.2 Benefits of affiliate marketing

Affiliate marketing is a business that brings mutual benefits to both the merchants and affiliate marketers. In case there is a network connecting the two, it also happens to benefit for connecting them. The affiliates gain by earning commissions whenever the product or service they are promoting is bought through their affiliate links. The amount of the commission can be fixed (PPC), pay-per-lead (registration) or even pay-per-sale. On the other hand, the merchants benefit by making more sales driven by affiliates and hence, more revenues. The affiliate networks also benefit by charging the merchants a small share of their revenue. The following are the advantages of affiliate marketing.

**1. It's a billion-dollar business opportunity**

Affiliate marketing is an industry that is capable of bringing its workers billions of dollars. In the current world, it has been flourishing fairly well. It has earned numerous people good money to sustain and develop them with their families. This seems to be its main advantage and is a huge incentive for you too to claim your share.

**2. It's a cheap business idea**

To join this business, it is pretty easy and fast since there are no entry barriers. What matters most is your decision to join and start. Start by creating a good affiliate website (not a must) based on a persuasive niche and find the products and services relevant to your market. After this, choose a good affiliate marketing program, pick the products and promote them on your website and social media accounts.

Additionally, investment costs are low compared to other industries. In the beginning, the costs are almost zero since you work online from your home or anywhere. You may only pay the ISP subscription and basic electricity costs. If you decide to set up your affiliate marketing site, you could pay some extra cash to get a domain, website design and hosting. And since you are a freelancer, there are no expenses in renting an office or buying inventories or hiring customer service.

**3. It requires no skills or expertise (because Practice Makes Perfect)**

To become an affiliate, you don't need to be a marketing expert or have excellent marketing skills. Anyone can start from scratch and learn through testing different organic and paid campaigns. Apply any marketing experience gained before as you examine what seems to be more lucrative. Then repeat the successful patterns while optimizing your affiliate site to get more good results.

## 4.Can be a good source of secondary income

You are not required to leave your current job so that you can join affiliate marketing. Instead, you can do it as a side-hustle and reap some extra income to add up to your salary.

## 5. Suitability and Flexibility

Affiliate marketing allows you to create numerous campaigns even on different websites and landing pages to market your affiliate links. This way, you can abandon the poorly performing sites and concentrate on optimizing the successful ones. At the same time, you don't have to stick to a single affiliate program. You can choose various products (even software) related to several lucrative niches and promote them regularly on your website.

When you have various types of products, they work to complement each other. Add attractive and diversified software and other products to your affiliate portfolio so when one fails, the others will be much easier and profitable to sell. This creates an opportunity for earning more income. In case a certain program fails to work for you, don't hesitate to drop it.

In addition, affiliate marketing provides you with a flexible working schedule. You work when you want and from any place you wish to. It allows you to go on vacations for the number of days you want and make time for any other important activities.

## 6. No need for customer service

Affiliate marketers do not suffer the problems of retaining customers through customer service. They care about commissions and in case of post-sale queries, they pass them to the merchant's customer service team. However, try to reply quickly to product-related questions under your posts in a detailed manner when you have a website for reviews.

## 7. It offers much freedom

Affiliate marketing provides flexible working environment as long as you have a reliable internet connection. You can work from literally anywhere. This sounds as a huge sense of freedom. In addition, there is no bureaucracy and no need to follow regulations of any company, such as providing weekly or monthly reports, managing team members, etc. Here, you follow your own rules, decide your dress code and other small habits that might be distractive. It also provides financial freedom where you decide which money to use where and for what reason. You reap the rewards all yourself.

## 8. Marketing materials are readily available

In most cases, merchants provide affiliates with all marketing materials needed to enhance promotion of their products. This may include banners, emails, among others.

## 9. It provides passive income

This is one of the strongest benefits of affiliate marketing. It allows you to make money while you sleep. You wake up in the morning and find some additional income in your account. Once you have done the hard work, you will get the fruits no matter where you are or what you are doing.

## 10. There is no limit to earning

There is no single time when you will be restricted to earn more money. The amount of revenue you earn depends on the number of sales you drive to the affiliate programs, which depends on how you market them. You can use an affiliate website, set up affiliate emails, use PPC campaigns, or even social media platforms. You can also combine paid and organic marketing strategies to drive more traffic to your affiliate promotion pages.

## 11. It's a sole proprietorship business

Mostly, affiliates work as freelancers to establish their business in the internet world. You don't even need a business permit to start and operate. You own your business alone, cover the costs such as laptop and internet connection, and enjoy the fruits alone.

## 12. Performance based revenues

Affiliate marketing will soon confirm what you are good at in the industry. For instance, it will verify whether you are a good content writer, video recorder, online review master, or PPC advertising guru. To succeed as an affiliate, it requires persistence and hard work. This is because it may take time to generate enough traffic to make you good money. The average time to earn satisfactory income would be 3 to 6 months. So, don't give up too early, give it time and the benefits will be yours to enjoy.

As we have seen, affiliate marketing is a sweet business to engage in. If done right and persistently, soon than later you will become successful in this business. As any other industry however, affiliate marketing has several disadvantages that come with it. Let's have a look at them!

## 4.3 Cons of affiliate marketing

### 1. You have no control over the affiliate marketing programs

It is logic that you do not own any affiliate marketing programs and therefore rely on the existing ones. This way, you are completely dependent on your networks or merchants, respecting their conditions and following their rules. Even if the competition of certain programs change over time, you can't alter the terms yourself. You can only communicate this to the merchants to adjust the discounts regarding given products. The merchants then decide to adjust or not.

## 2. You have no control over the competition

Due to the numerous benefits of affiliate marketing, many people are engaging in it, causing crowdedness in the online space. However, competition may vary depending on the type of industry and products being promoted. A significant disadvantage is that highly experienced affiliates from the same niche can make up severe competition. Nevertheless, this should not worry you. The main success factors of affiliate marketing are persistence and hard work. If you do this, soon you will succeed in this business and life.

## 3. You aren't free to create your own customer base

This is because after making the referral, the customer won't repeat buying through you again- you already made a connection. This is how most affiliate businesses operate, but you can still find others that offer recurring commission such as various JVZoo merchants, LiveChat Affiliate Program, and some of SaaS affiliate programs.

## 4. Revenue is not guaranteed

When you are paid for bringing traffic or sales, it is good in that you can earn a lot of money and at the same time, it can be a significant risk. This is because no one assures that it is easy working as an affiliate and you will start earning huge income when you begin it. It needs a lot of dedication, perseverance of any challenges, and more efforts into exploiting the opportunity. It is still difficult to predict the amount of money you will finally make.

## 5. Quantity rather than quality approach

Sometimes, affiliate marketing is accompanied by spammy marketing campaigns and misleading content for the shortsighted affiliates to earn some quick small incomes. If you happen to use these methods of false advertising, you can't go any far. You will soon lose your credibility and even endanger the reputation of your merchants. In addition, false campaigns break the cooperation from the merchant's side you don't get any commission.

However, if you focus on the long-term method and concentrate on quality rather than quantity, this business can bring you sustainable and recurring income. Be sincere and act reasonably to gain trust that will help you collaborate with the best merchants.

## 6. Affiliate links can be hijacked

Though it's rare and most affiliates won't do it, sometimes there appears cases of hijacking affiliate links to earn the affiliates' commission. When it happens, you can't get your money back. Therefore, you just need to hope that such a fraud won't aim at you.

## 7. Not everyone can do freelance jobs

Affiliate marketing and other freelance jobs requires a certain personality to feel comfortable working in such a style. Sometimes, it can make you feel blue due to stagnation and loneliness. However, there are ways to do away with such mental issues. You need not to stay more away from the people around you e.g. family and friends. You can find a working space in a place outside your home such as a coffee shop, co-working places, etc. and go there each day you want to work – like other freelancers.

It's my honest hope that the above pros and cons have helped you gain a deeper and better understanding of the nature of affiliate marketing business. Now you will be able to evaluate it better and decide whether it suits you or not. As you have noticed, the benefits outdo the disadvantages. Therefore, if you are serious and ready to start making extra cash with affiliate business, you can go ahead, find a lucrative niche, and join the best affiliate programs that fits you such as the LiveChat affiliate partner program and start earning right away. Following are the dos and don'ts for successful affiliate marketing.

## 4.4 The dos and don'ts in affiliate marketing

Affiliate marketing is a business that any person can do, and get awesome outcomes. Nevertheless, there are things that you can do and others you shouldn't do in order to enhance your success. To become an affiliate pro, the following are dos and don'ts to guide you along your way.

### 4.4.1 The Affiliate Marketing Do's

**1. Stick to your niche**

Most affiliates make the mistake of trying to promote too many diverse services and/or products hoping to earn more money. For the more established affiliates, this can work. However, if you are new in this industry, it is more advisable to focus on a few products relevant to your brand and niche. This builds an overlap between your audience and the products you are promoting, thereby increasing your chances of making high quality referrals and earn more revenues. For example, a fitness blogger would focus on promoting products such as vitamins, protein powders, workout equipment, and more, rather than just promoting the electronics and software products. Always try to stick to your niche and then include your related affiliate links in your posts.

**2. Provide compelling content**

All successful affiliates have one thing in common – creating compelling content! This is what attracts steady traffic and make them to return to their sites in the future. This is a great practice for all affiliates looking towards success in this business. Always ensure that you create high quality and engaging content that adds value to your visitors in your site, blog, email or video. This way, you build trust with your visitors as a reliable source of valuable information. When you do this consistently, then you can easily start promoting the related products and services, and drive more sales to your affiliate programs. Always try to use real examples while clearly guiding your audience on the benefits and how-to-use the products you are promoting.

### 3. Ensure you place affiliate links in appropriate positions

This may seem obvious to many people, but it happens that some affiliates don't do it properly. To earn commissions from the sales you drive, you must include the links for your audience to click in order to visit the merchant's website and purchase the product you are promoting. In all your promotional materials (blog posts, emails, videos, etc.), ensure you include enough affiliate links in appropriate positions such as the sidebar or at the end of the content. For example, whenever you write the brand name of the product or use relevant keywords, include a hyperlink under it. This makes it easy for your visitors to navigate to the referred website via these affiliate links, because the potential customers may not be able to read your post to the end. The more traffic you refer to an affiliate program, the higher your potential commissions.

### 4. Be patient

Success in affiliate marketing does not come in a night shift. Sometimes, it takes several months of testing and promoting different products to earn good commissions. Know the effective positions to place your affiliate links; this may take a lot of time to test too. Remove whatever that doesn't work and improve & increase the visibility and relevance of the CTAs in your social and blog posts. At the same time, learn the interests of your audience and the types of content that suits them the best. Persistent testing and enduring time will lead you to high revenues.

### 5. Work hand-in-hand with your affiliate manager

In most cases, you are paired up with an affiliate manager whenever you register for an affiliate program. This manager oversees the program and can guide you on the best effective practices. Additionally, you can get a wide range of resources designed to help you make successful referrals and earn huge income. Use all the available tools such as video ads, banner ads, and many more.    Then, ask your affiliate manager to help you with reliable practices and insightful ways to convert your traffic into sales. This way, you end up earning more income.

## 4.4.2 The Affiliate Marketing Don'ts

### 1. Do not be spammy

In order to maintain a steady traffic returning to your website, avoid posting spammy content and sending spammy emails. This refers to any information that is not relevant to your audience, or beyond their expectations. To ensure success in affiliate marketing business, make sure you post ONLY the content that is relevant and adds value to your audience. If you are spammy, you will possibly lose a significant amount of traffic and attract poor conversion rates. Even the affiliate program companies will become hesitant in working with you. So, avoid being spammy in your postings and emails.

### 2. Do not be salesy

Rather than trying to sell services/products on every post, focus on being educative and helpful. Explain your success stories with the services/products you are promoting. This is likely to result into more sales compared to simply explaining the advantages of the product and it suits everyone. Clearly depict the value and convince your audience that the particular product will be of great help to them, as it was to you. Again, try not to promote products on all posts and emails. Sometimes, you can post other informative content related to your niche to keep your audience engaged and excited.

### 3. Do not violate the terms of service of the affiliate program

In any affiliate program, you will find the terms of service upon which the program operates. You are required to agree with them before joining the program. These rules explains what you can and cannot do while promoting the products offered by the program. They may include referring your own sales, bidding on advertiser's branded keywords on search engines, etc. Violating any rule will have unfavorable consequences on you. Always ensure you follow these agreements and refer to them in case you are not sure about something. Once you neglect the terms, your affiliate program will email you to inform you that if you don't stop what you are doing, you risk the closure of your account and/or reversal of the commissions earned.


## 4.5 Myths about affiliate marketing

While a lot have been said about affiliate marketing, some of what's said are just myths and misconceptions to try distract you from doing this business successfully. If you consider these rumors, you might find yourself giving up soon or later after starting it. This is to mean that you are not supposed to believe them in any case. Be dumb and blind about the myths and you will become successful in this business. Let's see what are some of the myths about affiliate marketing.

### 1. Affiliate marketing is easy

Most people misunderstand the affiliate marketing business as an easy way of making money online. They think it's a cakewalk. For experienced marketers, this could bear some bit of truth. However, it requires a lot of time and hard work, as well as optimal and right techniques to beat the competition in affiliate marketing. And as in most industries, there are no shortcuts to achieve success. In fact, a recent popular survey has revealed that only about 0.6% of affiliates have been remarkably successful. So, don't think it's a walk in the park, work to attract success.

### 2. Ample traffic means abundant revenues

Many of the new affiliate marketers assume that their primary focus should be directing traffic to their affiliate links, then converting this traffic into customers. It could be reliable and better to depend on the number of visitors converted into customers rather than depending on the number of your site's visitors. Affiliate marketing is a skillful business for example for the level of appealing that the product brings, rather than the number of people who viewed the product. Always try to advertise your affiliate products fully in a pleasing and significant way.

### 3. Affiliate marketing is all about luck not expertise

Most people who fail to understand the reason behind another person's success in any field tend to believe that certain features, which include chance and luck, rule success. However, this doesn't apply to affiliate marketing, where optimum understanding of how this business operates can help address many mistakes that hinder your success. Some people advertise their products in an irrelevant fashion that hardly attracts sales.

For success, you need to put yourself in the shoes of your prospective buyers to coordinate your adverts with things that the customers are searching for. This could include efficient keyword research and Search Engine Optimization (SEO). It may require some experience and expertise to ensure you convert your traffic into purchasers.

### 4. Social media popularity guarantees affiliate marketing success

Social networking assists you to advertise and promote your products without expenses. However, having high popularity on social media doesn't mean that the products you sell will be bought and bring you income. Sometimes, using popular and famous people in advertising your products can help a lot in bringing traffic to your site. Many consumers understand that quality and product description is more important than the marketer. In some cases, you can use paid advertising to increase your social reach. But don't be fooled to think that this will definitely equate to the level of your success.

### 5. Affiliate Marketing is all about advertising top notch products and niches

This may sometimes sound true since most products belong to certain groups of popular niches. However, it is not necessarily that the chief attraction of each customer is limited to only these top niches. Even though those popular niches are thriving in the affiliate business, they are not easy to dwell in since the competition is quite high. No matter the popularity of the products, a competent affiliate marketer can be able to bring new identity to certain rare products and end up boosting their success rates.

### 6. It solely depends on the content published on the website

It is really true that affiliate marketing relies on the quality of content provided on the website. However, this is not all that matters. Quality content key for affiliate success and it is only aimed to provide all product's information to the prospective buyers. At the same time, it is crucial to regularly update your website with fresh and exciting information that doesn't disrupt your visitors. Use unique and interesting images within the articles to make your website stand out from the rest in the eyes of your visitors. This way, you might be able to prompt more visitors to buy the products you are promoting.

It is not advisable to advertise a product one time only and leave it to communicate itself. Ensure you update the content regularly to foster success in your affiliate marketing business.

### 7. You are too late to join

Some people tend to think that they are very late to join affiliate marketing and start making money from it. Even your friends might discourage you from engaging in this business. This could be because they don't want more competition and therefore they tell you that it's not worth the hassle. However, affiliate marketing is ever open for anyone to join. New opportunities are created on a daily basis for even the new players to make money through affiliate marketing. So, go ahead as early as now, join this business, and provide value to maximize your revenues.

## 8. It needs a lot of cash to begin

This is one of the most persistent myths about affiliate marketing. They say that if you don't have money to spend on media purchases, you should not bother. However, it is very possible to attain success with a tight budget or even without spending a dime. Succeeding in affiliate marketing is dependent on your inputs (efforts and money), like any other business. But it is not necessarily that you have to have a lot of money to start.

## 9. It is only for specialists with advanced business degrees

Affiliate marketing is not necessarily a job to be pursued by professional marketers with an academic relation to business studies. Rather than technical business skills, it requires more creative and intuitive skills of what words are used in daily life. Enthusiastic people with skills and grit for the job can use their brain (rather than qualifications) to become highly skillful affiliate marketers.

## 10. It is a dead end

It is a joke that some think that affiliate marketing has reached a dead end. This is because there are numerous trends that resulted in to reasonable variation compared to when affiliate marketing was first hypothesized. There have been placed certain specifications and standards that enhance the relevance and productivity of this business. Google and other search engines have optimized their Search Engine Result Pages (SERPs) to rank low those websites that fail to adhere to their rules and regulations. Banner ads are also diminishing and being replaced with text ads since they don't go very well with a good number of electronic devices used in the modern world. all these changes imply the improvements in this industry rather than its demolition.

## 11. Affiliate Marketing was established by Amazon

The Amazon Associates program was founded in 1996 and people erroneously think that affiliate marketing started this way. However, the father of affiliate marketing – William J. Tobin – started his own affiliate program in 1989 on the Prodigy Network to advertise his company PC Gifts & Flowers. In addition, CDNow launched its BuyWeb program in 1994, preceding the Amazon Associates program. This is a clear indication that Amazon was not the founder of affiliate marketing.

## 12. It's a "Get Rich Fast" System

Everyone would like to hit the gold on their first try. Some super affiliate marketers are making tons of money every month (such as $100,000+). This is much possible for any affiliate.

However, this doesn't happen overnight, those successful affiliates really worked off their asses to reach to the point they are today. If you are blogger, you may start making sales after the third to sixth months mark. While it is not that easy to start and earn huge money quickly, success in affiliate marketing requires a lot of dedication, effort, planning and time. This can't be called instant gratification.

### 13. You need to come from a specific T1 country

The fact is that T1 countries such as UK, USA and Canada provide traffic that is more valuable. This makes affiliates from other countries such as India and Africa think they can't make it in this business. No one controls where he/she is born. However, anyone can learn to make money online and take rightful actions to start earning as an affiliate, regardless of where you come from or live.

## 4.6 FAQs in Affiliate Marketing

## 4.61 General Questions

### What is Affiliate Marketing?

Affiliate Marketing is a kind of online marketing business that allows affiliates to earn commissions by recommending or referring a buyer to the services or products from the merchant. Look at the full introduction in the first chapter of this book.

### Why engage in affiliate marketing?

Affiliate marketing offers one of the best promising ways to make passive income online. It allows you the freedom to work when you want, from where you want, with or without paid assistance, and lets you to choose whether to work part time or full time. As you have seen above, there are more advantages than disadvantages of this business.

### How do you promote affiliate links?

Most people think that it is only through a website that you can do affiliate marketing and succeed. While having a website/blog may foster the success rate, you can promote your affiliate links through various other methods. This includes:

- Using a newsletter or email list.
- Social media marketing, such as Pinterest, Facebook, Twitter, etc.
- Posting in comment sections of forums and other blogs.
- Using digital products such as eBooks.
- YouTube videos and live streaming.

You can use one or several of the above methods to attract multiple-streamed income.

### What are the criticisms against affiliate marketing?

The most common and serious criticism of this industry is the abuse of affiliate links. this is triggered by the increase of affiliates who makes all efforts to maximize their revenue. Don't be fooled to use unethical methods or spam people because you have learned some basics of affiliate marketing and just want to reach a wider audience to make more cash. This will make you quit soon since you can't get any results. Take time to learn the successful affiliate marketing techniques and you won't have this issue.

### How do you earn money as an affiliate?

As an affiliate marketer, you make money by referring people to purchase products or services from a merchant. You can be connected to the seller through an affiliate network such as ShareASale, JVZoo, among others.

### How do I sign up for an affiliate program?

Simply look for the best affiliate opportunities around the net, register and start promoting their products on your website or using other methods to start making money. Some examples of good affiliate programs are the Amazon Associates, CJ, ShareASale, and Wealthy Affiliates programs.

### What types of services and products can I promote?

Affiliate marketing allows you to promote any products and services that you deem relevant to your niche and available in a certain affiliate program. You can sell non-physical products such as software, eBooks, online tools, online course, membership sites, among others, or physical products, which are more straightforward – such as electronics, clothing, home and improvements, etc. You only need to ensure that your services and products are relevant to your niche and target market, as well as providing solutions to people's problems. You might also want to consider the affordability of the products you are promoting to ensure capability of driving sales and earning income.

### How much time should I devote to my business?

No precise amount of time that you are required to invest in your business. It literally depends on your plan and diary. You can spend 3 hours per week or up to 4 hours daily. But the fact is, investing more time in your business will make you see good results faster and make more money.

### Do I have to pay for affiliate marketing training?

It is not necessary for you to pay for training, but it is recommended. In the modern world, almost all info you need to succeed in online marketing can be attained freely from the internet. Nevertheless, it will take you lots of time to research and acquire this information. It is also possible to get false info and scams on the net. This is why it is recommended for serious affiliates (especially beginners) to find systematic affiliate training. The best resources and training materials are offered at a cost but most guarantee you to get your money back and this will enhance your success in this business.

**How much income can I generate through this business?**

There is no limit to earning through affiliate marketing; you can make as much money as you want! The earning potential of marketers and merchants is truly huge (some make up to $100k every monthly). However, it requires a lot of learning, dedication, time and it may need you some money to earn more money.

**Can I sell or promote services and products that I've never used?**

Yes, you can promote any products and services even the ones that you have never used. However, you need to give a well-researched and completely honest review of the products you are promoting or selling. Buying and using the product yourself will help you give a comprehensive and high quality review, but it is really hard and expensive to purchase all the items you promote (especially if you are just starting out).

## 4.6.2 Niche-based Questions

**What is a niche?**

A niche is a profitable and specialized corner of the market, which includes the target audience interested in the products and services you are offering/promoting. Choosing a niche includes identifying the kind of people you want to help to solve their problems and meet their needs and wants.

**How should I find the right niche?**

To find a good niche, you don't need to be an expert in any relevant field. You just need to have good research skills and if you don't have, you will learn as soon as you start. In order to find a lucrative niche, you will want to consider these four things:

1. Does it revolve around your passion/hobby?
2. Is it specific?
3. Is related content readily accessible?
4. Is it a profitable one?
5. Is it in high demand?
6. Are there marketers promoting products in this niche?
7. Are there products to promote in this niche?
8. What are the trends in this niche?

Once you have found positive answers to the above questions, then you have found yourself a lucrative niche.

### 4.6.3 Website-based Questions

**What is the difference between free and paid hosting? Which one is better?**

Website hosting gives you the chance to have an actual address/domain for your website/blog. You can get a free hosting, which provides you with a subdomain such as yourdomain.wix.com, yourdomain.wordpress.com, among others. You can also use paid hosting such as bluehost.com, ipage.com, or WordPress, which gives you free site builders and templates to make you the website you want. Paid hosting is recommended since it gives you the full control of your website and likely to rank better. However, you do not own the free subdomains fully.

**Do I need to be a tech person or have coding skills to do affiliate marketing?**

With the modern technology, you can easily make an attractive and professional website with no coding skills. So, it is not necessarily that you should have any coding skills. One of the most popular CMS is WordPress, which allows you to manage and edit your website in their user-friendly interface without any coding. Another one is SiteRubix that uses WordPress CMS and allows you to design your website in several minutes.

**Should my homepage be a static page or my blogs list?**

A static page is highly recommended since it allows you to inform your visitors clearly about what they should expect from your site and whether it suits them. On the other hand, using a blogroll as your homepage fails to serve the primary purpose of telling your visitors all about your website. Most people who do this are lazy and don't know what to include in their homepages. People need easy and straightforward navigation to quickly understand what your website entails. Make sure you deliver a clear message of what you are offering to your visitors and include CTA buttons to ease the navigation.

### 4.6.4 Content Formation Questions

**How long should a good article or post be?**

There is no definite length that a post should be. However, as Neil Patel points out here, longer contents is usually better for high ranking on the SERPs. Most of the highest ranking posts are usually above 2000 words. Do not mistake by thinking that people don't want or have time to read long articles. Lengthy informative content attracts more shares, backlinks, and trust by search engines like Google. But this doesn't mean that short contents don't deliver value.

**Can I transform other people's posts and publish them as my own?**

Yes. Search engines will consider it as original content if you translate it manually yourself. And since there are numerous ways to translate content, it is very hard to detect content from other sources. Don't make the mistake of using translation software like Google Translate as the content will be of low quality and may be detected by search engines. Provide original and unique content to enhance long-term benefits from this online business.

## Must I be a good writer to produce good content?

No. Though it's somehow advantageous, being a writer doesn't guarantee you the ability to write good content for your website. Content writing is very different compared to books and composition writing. To improve your incomes, you need to write conversion-based contents and naturally include relevant keywords and affiliate links. Whether you are good in writing or not, you can create attractive content that converts your readers into buyers of the products you are promoting, and end up making huge passive income.

## How frequently should I publish a blog post?

This depends much on your time schedule. Most people normally post one post per week, but it can be even better if you post more often. If you don't post regularly however, it will take you longer to see good results with affiliate marketing.

## Can I outsource the creation of my content or blog posts?

Yes, affiliate marketing lets you outsource content creation by hiring other experienced writers to write you the content. However, do it only after you have seen some good results and are sure that it will bring more money. This is because it is not always easy and cheap to obtain high quality and converting content. When you decide to do so, make sure you give clear description and instructions to your writers so that the outsourced content can make you real money.

## Can I duplicate info from various sites & combine them in one post?

No. When you do this, you risk being penalized by Google and other search engines. This results in poor rankings of your site and therefore you get less organic traffic. Rather than posting content that's not yours, ensure your content is original, unique and adds value for you to rank high and make more money.

**Pro Tip:** The best way to quote content from other sites is taking screenshots rather than copying it directly.

## Can I publish the same post again in various locations of my site?

No. It is not acceptable since the search engines will consider it as duplicated content. This makes it to rank very low, and hence not advisable.

## How many keywords should I use per article?

You should always use one main keyword or keyword phrase in the entire article and include its variations within the post.

## 4.6.5 Website Development Questions

**What is the best traffic source for my website?**

Organic search is the best traffic that comes through the search engines when your posts are ranked. This is because not only is it free, but also ensures you passive and constant traffic once your posts are ranked high. According to Convertkit research, organic search is the leading traffic source for successful affiliate marketers.

**What is the best strategy to grow your audience?**

Social Media is the best and most suitable way to grow your audience. This is because it is among the most common platforms used by people to communicate and attract audience.


## Chapter Five: Trends in affiliate marketing in 2019

Affiliate marketing is a constantly changing business, similar to other industries. To maximize your overall ROI and ensure wise usage of your cash, I recommend you to stay up-to-date with the ever-changing trends. As you plan your affiliate marketing practices this 2019, keep these trends in mind:

### 5.1 Affiliate Marketing trends in 2019

### 1. Sturdy product reviews and review websites are still king.

Writing highly qualified and strong product reviews and including their keywords is still on top of the game of affiliate marketing. This is because people search for specific product reviews and testimonials before making a purchase. As Neil Patel (a successful & famous affiliate marketer) points out, well-written product reviews and review sites will continue to be a huge trend in affiliate marketing in 2019 and later on.

### 2. Increased focus on imageries and audiovisual content.

Nowadays, writing convincing content isn't the only thing necessary to succeed in affiliate marketing. Affiliates are becoming more and more creative every day in their messaging by use of pictures, videos, slideshows, courses, demos, live streaming, among other ways. This makes it more easy for them to attract huge audience and earn more commissions. Additionally, it helps in broadening the number of potential promotional and affiliate opportunities.

### 3. Voice search is on the rise.

With the increasing of assistance of companies like Siri, and adoption of smart devices such as the Amazon Alexa and Google Home, voice search is becoming more effective and necessary for affiliates. You need to optimize your campaigns for more natural speech patterns and long-tail keywords.

## 4. Expanding your portfolio.

Affiliate marketers are continually diversifying their portfolios to include different merchants and affiliate platforms, rather than relying exclusively on a single model such as the Amazon Associates. This has also been influenced by the signs of Amazon to branch into smaller and more brick-and-mortar stores.

## 5. Appropriate affiliate staffing is more crucial than ever.

The act of recruiting the proper affiliate resources is becoming very important than it has ever been. This is collinear with the continuous growth of affiliate marketers, merchants and the entire affiliate industry. Rather than having numerous random and general niche web publishers, having a smaller number of highly qualified and targeted mobile affiliates and web publishers will still prove to be more effective.

## 6. Ecommerce stores are entering the game.

Ecommerce retailers are continually showing interest in affiliate marketing to enhance their efforts of lead generation. Many of them are even starting their individual affiliate programs via networks such as Shareasale and Linkshare, thereby increasing the opportunities for new and existing affiliates. This shows how great the potential growth of this affiliate marketing business is.

## 7. Affiliate networks are increasing.

In order to see long-term financial achievement through affiliate marketing, it requires special skills to be set. However, many online merchants lack the proper team and resources to do it appropriately, probably inside an office. This has resulted into an increase in the number of agencies that specialize in providing affiliate-marketing services. This trend is very likely to continue throughout this 2019 and in the future.

## 8. Growing influence of Facebook ads and other marketing tools.

Most affiliates are gradually using Facebook ads, Twitter ads, and Google ads, among others in their efforts to reach larger audience. Facebook ads is specifically being continually used, probably because of its splendid exhaustive targeting opportunities and capabilities to enhance remarketing campaigns. While advertising through Facebook Messenger, keep in mind that Facebook is not always friendly to affiliate marketing and occasionally bans some advertisers. At the same time, Amazon inhibits advertisements of their affiliate links on social media. So, ensure you **watch your campaigns closely**.

## 5.2 Mobile Affiliate Marketing Trends

With the continuous growth & popularity of mobile usage, there are several mobile affiliate-marketing trends to keep in mind. This starts with what some people may call 'general/obvious', - optimizing your affiliate site and platforms for mobile devices. This is triggered by Google's efforts to ensure best options in search by tailoring the results provided to the consumers/users. About 64% of all paid Google search clicks comes from mobile devices. Optimizing for mobiles will help improve the effectiveness of your campaigns and maximize the usage of your paid ads. In addition, you can use mobile-only offers to increase your reach, influence on the growing mobile audience, and attract more leads.

From the above trends, you can see that affiliate marketing is a continuously growing and evolving industry. And as an affiliate, you need to evolve your marketing strategies to ensure success in this business and time.

## 5.3 Affiliate Marketing Takeaways

Affiliate marketing is a lucrative business for you and anyone else to engage in and make good money online. Numerous affiliates have been successful in this business to the extent of making 6-7 figure income through it. It is not always easy to succeed, however. It requires continuous dedication and persistence to make the most out of it. To foster your success, there are three important resources that you Need-to-Have.

- To start with, you need to pick the right niche that you will focus all your affiliate efforts on. Niche selection is a long process, I have discussed it deeply in Chapter Two.

- Then, you need to set up your affiliate website. Make sure you optimize it for both mobile and computer devices for better SEO rankings. I have explained its importance above too.
- And finally, you require to write a systematic plan. You can spend all the time you want to map out the best strategies and marketing strategies to make sure it will bear the expected results once implemented. This is how you can make huge income through affiliate marketing.

# Chapter Six: Bonuses

## 6.1 (Bonus 1): Ten Best Tips for Successful Facebook Marketing 2019

Facebook is the number one social media website that lets friends connect freely and share information online. In addition, this platform allows space to enable businesses and affiliate marketers increase their reach and drive more sales. This is what is called Facebook Marketing and it is rapidly growing in number of marketers who advertise their products and services on the platform. Big corporations and small businesses are using this powerful marketing tool to develop their brand identity, keep customers informed and increase their reach. It also helps them increase clicks to their websites as well as sales and revenues. However, succeeding in marketing through Facebook is not a walk in the park. It requires certain techniques to enhance the effectiveness of your marketing plan.

Below are the ten best tips to boost your success in Facebook Marketing.

## 1) Have a well-defined goal and plan

Having clear objectives for using Facebook in your marketing activities and a strategy designed to attain the set goals is crucial to every Facebook marketer. The goals could be to upsurge the sales made through Facebook by a certain percentage within the following defined time (e.g. 4 months). To achieve such a goal, you can plan the activities to be; post creation every morning, use daily images, and encourage users to share their photos and comments. Make sure the activities are aimed to achieving the set goals. Goals also help in evaluating the level of success attained in a specific period.

## 2) Build a humanoid voice for your brand

Facebook users are humans and like talking to other humans rather than impersonal communication. If you can't manage your Facebook page, find a person who will help you write in a real and likeable tone suitable for your business. Let them express different things in their own words rather than using the business's official lines so they can sound really personal.

## 3) Inspire users to comment and respond fast

Always encourage users to give their opinions regarding your posts or post comments regarding your company. In case they post a comment, be ready to reply quickly before 24 hours are over. If you don't respond, you will weaken your users' willingness to engage with you and your posts, and soon they will leave you.

## 4) Ensure you post frequently

Social media platforms differ from other types of media such as television, magazines, web pages, etc. in that they are designed for regular updates. In fact, Facebook users check their pages more than twenty five times a week. Therefore, you need to keep posting new material every now and then, at least once a day. But when you have interesting content, post it and try to examine how frequently your followers wants to get your information.

## 5) Use images and audiovisual materials

Videos and photos are the major component of the appealing Facebook. It is recommended to use them often to ensure your friends and followers are always entertained and engaged. People use Facebook for fun and therefore, you should use interactive materials such as contests, games, offers, surveys, among others to keep your followers amused. You can also give giveaways and discounts to entice more follows on your page.

## 6) Cultivate for your relationships

Building a good strong relationship with other users may not be easy and takes time. So, be patient and keep engaging frankly in conversations, offer helpful content, and come up with rewards for your honest customers to enhance good relations.

### 7) Never use the hard-sell tactic for Facebook marketing

Many people see Facebook as an amusing social space that allows friends to share and view information, status, photos, videos, etc. It is recommended to engage in conversations with your community instead of acting like an outsider who sells by force. If you use the hard-sell techniques such as posting frequently on a specific service or product, using advertising slogans, providing products' lists, among others, without any interrelated conversation, you are most likely to get huge numbers of unfollows who may even share negative comments and reviews regarding your business. So, make sure you don't use Facebook for the hard sell.

### 8) Advertise your posts on Facebook

Facebook allows page owners to have their specific posts reach a given number of users and increase the impression on the particular post at a flat cost. It is not necessarily that users will see your posts on their news feed for the health of your fans. A fan might be looking at their news feed at the time you are posting, but there is no guarantee that they will see it, since other posts could swamp their news feed. This is why it is recommended to use paid ads by Facebook.

When you pay for your post on Facebook, you are at least sure that it will reach some targeted audience and probably, they will complete the action you are calling them to perform. This could include liking your page, reading a certain story, visiting your website, buying a certain product, among others. Once a campaign is over, you will have gotten more likes to your page, more traffic to your site, more post reach, and more sales which would result into more revenue.

You can choose to use the normal Facebook ads, Sponsored Posts, or Promoted ads to advertise your posts on Facebook. All these plans are reasonably priced but the cost, CPCs and CTRs may differ from one plan to another.

### 9) Advertise your Facebook page

It is wise to promote your Facebook page via your business. This will help to combine social media marketing with other traditional marketing tactics. Put your Facebook address on your business card, letterhead, store, advertisements, email signatures, and website. This will help attract more people to your Facebook page and give you a wider social reach.

### 10) Make good use of Facebook Insights

Facebook provides information about your page likers and their demographics through the so-called "Facebook Insights". Knowing your audience's characteristics (including age, gender, location, interests, etc.) can help you design your offers and posts to meet their specific interests and needs. And once you do this, there are high chances of conversions and sales.

In conclusion, Facebook is a great channel used by numerous businesses to market their services and goods. In fact, many companies have earned huge incomes by using Facebook marketing to generate more sales. With the above ten tips, you too can use Facebook to market your items and services, attract sales and earn more income from your business. You can also build your Facebook community to reach more people. All these will help you keep your customers informed, develop your brand identity, increase your reach, and raise your revenues.

## 6.2 (Bonus 2): 50+ Best Affiliate Networks and 30+ Marketing Blogs to Join In 2019

In the modern affiliate marketing space, there is high competition from thousands of websites that offer different categories of this service to both merchants and marketers. However, it sometimes becomes hard to identify the affiliate networks that genuinely pay for successful sales driven by the affiliates. This is because there is an increase in fake platforms that make you waste a lot of your time and resources while anticipating for huge incomes.

That's why I have listed the 50+ best affiliate marketing networks that genuinely reward you for your promotion efforts. You might want to consider the privacy policies and terms of service offered by any network before joining them. At the same time, it's recommendable to look for different reviews about the specific platform you wish to join so that you can see different user reviews. This will help you to join ONLY the affiliate network that has the great potentiality of making huge income.

Let's now dive into the affiliate network list of 2019.

### 6.2.1 Best Affiliate Network List In 2019

1. PeerFly

2. ShareASale

3. Rakuten

4. Wide Markets

5. MaxBounty

6. Affiliate Window (AWIN)

7. Amazon

8. ClickBank

9. CJ Affiliate

10. VigLink

11. JVZoo

12. TradeDoubler

13. CrakRevenue

14. Commission Factory

15. Target Affiliates

16. AvanGante (2Checkout)

17. AvantLink

18. FlexOffers

19. Commission Junction

20. Partnerstack

21. eBay Partner Network

22. AdCombo

23. SellHealth

24. Market Health

25. Forex Club

26. 8Binary.com

27. ImpactRadius

28. RevenueWire

29. Olavivo

30. MoreNiche

31. AffiBank

32. Sendible

33. ClickFunnels

34. SEMRush

35. LeadPages

36. Shopify.com

37. StudioPress

38. ConvertKit

39. Cupid.com

40. FriendFinder

41. Regal Assets

42. Flywheel

43. URL Profiler

44. DreamHost

45. BlueHost

46. WP Engine

47. StudioPress

48. LinkConnector

49. Skim Links

50. Mailerlite

51. Casino Blasters

52. iAffiliates

53. Betfair Affiliates

54. eHarmony

55. Colmex Pro

## 6.2.2 Best affiliate marketing blogs to follow in 2019

These are the best blogs that comprise of information and guidance regarding affiliate marketing. Following these blogs will help you improve your affiliate marketing knowledge so that you can realize more ways to maximize your operation tactics. Here is the list:

1. Shawn Collins | Affiliate Marketing Blog

2. ShoeMoney - Jeremy Schoemaker

3. Niche Pursuits

4. Affiliate Summit Blog – Affiliate Summit

5. Deadbeat Super Affiliate

6. Tricia Meyer

7. Affbuzz.com

8. CharlesNgo.com

9. Affilorama | Affiliate Marketing Blog

10. Affilinet Inside | Affiliate Marketing Blog

11. Work In My Pajamas

12. ShareASale Blog » Affiliates News

13. Entrepreneur » Affiliate Marketing

14. Affiliate Marketing Blog by Geno Prussakov

15. Mobidea Academy | Affiliate Marketing Training, Guides & Tips

16. AvantLink | Affiliate Marketing Best Practices and News

17. Affiliate Marketing with Missy Ward

18. Marketing Land » Affiliate Marketing

19. Cloudways Blog » Affiliate Marketing

20. Reddit » Affiliate Marketing

21. Rethink Commerce » Blog Affiliates

22. Smart Insights » Affiliate marketing

23. Flipboard » Affiliate Marketing

24. Business 2 Community » Affiliate Marketing

25. ShoutMeLoud | Blogging & Affiliate marketing

26. The Drum - Affiliate Marketing

27. Affposts

28. Entrepreneurs-Journey.com - Yaro Starak

29. Human Proof Designs

30. FMTC Blog

31. DigitalSeoGuide » Affiliate-Marketing

32. Acceleration Partners » Affiliate Marketing

33. 2 Create a Website Blog

34. Webicy Webmaster Forum » Affiliate Marketing

35. affiliaXe | Affiliate Marketing Blog

There you have them- the best affiliate networks and marketing blogs in 2019. If you haven't joined any specific affiliate network presented in this list, you can try and register for them to increase income from your website or online business. Additionally, you can subscribe to the above affiliate marketing blogs so as to learn more regarding this topic and its trends over time. They provide high quality and helpful information to help you achieve your business dreams.

www.ingramcontent.com/pod-product-compliance
Lightning Source LLC
Chambersburg PA
CBHW030526220526
45463CB00007B/2744